Flask Web Framework

Building a Flask web app using Bootstrap and an SQLite database.

A complete beginner-friendly learning path.

MARK JOHN LADO

While every precaution has been taken in the preparation of this book, the publisher and the authors assume no responsibility for errors or omissions, or for damages resulting from the use of the information contained herein.

No part of this publication may be reproduced, distributed, or transmitted in any form or by any means, including photocopying, recording, or other electronic or mechanical methods, without the prior written permission of the author, except in the case of brief quotations embodied in critical reviews and certain other noncommercial uses permitted by copyright law.

All trademarks, service marks, trade names, logos, and icons (collectively, "Marks") appearing in this publication are the property of their respective owners. This publication may contain references to various Marks for informational and illustrative purposes only. The use of such Marks herein does not constitute or imply any endorsement or sponsorship by the respective owners of those Marks, nor does it grant any license, express or implied, to use any Marks. Any unauthorized use of any Marks is strictly prohibited.

.

DEDICATION

This book is dedicated to all the aspiring developers and students who seek to harness the power of web development to create meaningful and impactful digital experiences. To those who are eager to learn, explore, and push the boundaries of what is possible with Flask, this work is for you. May it serve as a stepping stone toward mastering the skills needed to build robust, dynamic web applications and inspire you to pursue excellence in the ever-evolving field of technology.

I also dedicate this book to the countless mentors, educators, and fellow developers who have shared their knowledge, patience, and insights over the years. Your contributions to the learning community have been invaluable, and it is through your guidance that many, including myself, have come to realize the immense potential that lies within the world of web development.

ACKNOWLEDGMENTS

I would like to express my deepest gratitude to everyone who contributed to the completion of this book. First and foremost, my sincere thanks go to my family for their unwavering support, encouragement, and patience throughout this journey. Your belief in me has been a constant source of motivation.

I am also profoundly grateful to the many educators and mentors who have shaped my understanding of web development and programming. Your guidance and expertise have laid the foundation for this book's content and structure. Special thanks to the Flask community and open-source contributors whose resources, tutorials, and discussions provided the knowledge and inspiration needed to bring this work to life.

To my peers, thank you for your feedback and constructive criticism that helped refine the ideas within these pages. Lastly, a heartfelt thank you to all the readers—your pursuit of knowledge drives me to continue contributing to this ever-growing field of technology.

Table of Contents

Chapter 1: Introduction to Flask and Web Development

1.1 What is Flask?

Flask is a lightweight and flexible web framework written in Python that allows developers to build web applications with minimal overhead. Originally developed by Armin Ronacher in 2010 as part of the Pocoo project, Flask was designed to be simple yet powerful, giving developers the freedom to structure applications according to their needs. Flask is often categorized as a microframework because it does not include default tools like form validation, database abstraction layers, or authentication mechanisms out of the box. However, this minimalism is by design—it encourages developers to integrate only the components they require, leading to highly customizable solutions.

In real-world applications, Flask has been widely adopted for prototyping, developing RESTful APIs, and even powering full-scale websites and administrative dashboards. For instance, organizations such as Netflix and Lyft have used Flask to build microservices, benefiting from its modularity and seamless integration with other Python libraries. In academic settings, Flask is often preferred due to its shallow learning curve and strong alignment with Python programming practices commonly taught in university courses.

1.2 Advantages of Using Flask for Small to Medium Web Applications

One of the most compelling reasons to choose Flask for small to medium web applications is its simplicity. Flask allows developers to create a fully functioning web server in just a few lines of code, making it ideal for classroom demonstrations, student projects, and rapid application development. Unlike more monolithic frameworks, Flask's minimal structure encourages developers to understand the foundational principles of web development, such as HTTP routing, request handling, and template rendering.

Another advantage lies in Flask's flexibility. Developers are not forced into a specific project layout or rigid conventions. Instead, they can choose how to structure their codebase based on the size and complexity of the application. This flexibility makes Flask ideal for developing modular applications that can grow over time. Moreover, the extensive Python ecosystem allows easy integration with libraries for machine learning (like TensorFlow), data analysis (like Pandas), or database management (like SQLAlchemy).

Educational institutions also favor Flask due to its clear syntax and compatibility with modern development practices. For instance, Flask can be integrated with Bootstrap (for responsive UI design) or JavaScript frameworks (for dynamic front-end interactivity), thereby offering students a comprehensive, real-world development experience.

1.3 Overview of the MVC Pattern

At the heart of modern web application development lies the Model-View-Controller (MVC) pattern, a design paradigm that separates application logic into three interconnected components. This separation of concerns not only enhances maintainability but also promotes scalability and collaboration among development teams.

In the context of Flask, the **Model** typically represents the data layer—handled via SQLite or an Object-Relational Mapper (ORM) like SQLAlchemy. The **View** comprises the user interface, defined using HTML templates enhanced with Jinja2, Flask's default templating engine. The **Controller** acts as the intermediary, processing incoming requests, interacting with the model, and rendering the appropriate view.

A practical example would be a university course management system. The model would consist of tables representing students, courses, and instructors stored in an SQLite database. The views would include pages that display course lists, registration forms, or academic records. The controller would manage operations such as registering a student for a course, validating inputs, and updating the database—all while ensuring the correct view is rendered based on user interaction.

1.4 Flask vs Django (Brief Comparison)

When choosing a web framework, one common question arises: should I use Flask or Django? While both are written in Python and share many underlying technologies, they differ significantly in philosophy and usage.

Django is a full-stack framework designed to handle all aspects of web development, from authentication to admin interfaces, out of the box. It follows the "batteries-included" philosophy, offering a lot of built-in functionality. This makes Django ideal for large-scale applications where rapid development and standard conventions are essential. However, for beginners, the learning curve can be steeper, and the rigid project structure may obscure the underlying mechanics.

Flask, in contrast, adopts a minimalist approach. It provides the core tools needed to build a web app and leaves the rest to the developer's discretion. This makes Flask more transparent and beginner-friendly. It allows students and junior developers to learn the basics of HTTP requests, routing, and data handling without the abstraction layers that Django imposes. In real-world terms, Flask is often chosen for APIs, microservices, or applications requiring custom logic and UI, whereas

Django is preferred for enterprise-scale content management systems or applications requiring built-in admin dashboards.

1.5 Installing Python and pip

Before diving into Flask development, it is essential to have Python and pip installed on your system. Python is the programming language that underpins Flask, while pip is the package manager used to install Flask and other dependencies.

To install Python, visit the official website https://www.python.org/downloads/ and download the version compatible with your operating system. Ensure that the option to "Add Python to PATH" is checked during installation to enable command-line usage.

After installation, open your terminal or command prompt and verify the installation with the following commands:

```
python --version
pip --version
```

These should return the installed versions of Python and pip, respectively. If not, you may need to manually add Python to your system's PATH environment variable.

To install Flask, you can use the following command:

```
pip install Flask
```

This command downloads and installs Flask and its dependencies from the Python Package Index (PyPI). For better project management, it is recommended to use a virtual environment. You can create one by running:

```
python -m venv venv
```

```
source venv/bin/activate   # On Windows use:
venv\Scripts\activate
pip install Flask
```

This setup allows you to isolate project dependencies, making your development environment cleaner and more manageable. For educators and students working in labs or shared computers, this approach is also practical for avoiding conflicts between different Python packages or projects.

Conclusion

Chapter 1 provides the foundational knowledge necessary to begin developing with Flask. It introduces not only the technical framework but also the contextual relevance of Flask in both academic and professional environments. By understanding the MVC architecture, the advantages of Flask's lightweight design, and how to set up the development environment, students and educators are better prepared to engage in deeper technical discussions and hands-on project work. As the following chapters build upon this foundation, the reader will transition from theory to practice, culminating in the creation of dynamic, database-driven web applications using Flask and modern front-end technologies.

Chapter 2: Setting Up Your Development Environment

2.1 Installing Flask

Establishing a robust and organized development environment is a fundamental step for any Information Technology student or educator aspiring to build reliable web applications using Flask. Flask, as previously introduced, is a minimalist framework that allows developers to create web applications efficiently, but its power is only fully realized when set up correctly in a dedicated workspace. The installation of Flask begins with ensuring that Python and pip, Python's package installer, are already installed. As Flask is not bundled with Python by default, it must be explicitly added to your working environment.

To begin, create a dedicated directory where your project files will reside. Using a terminal or command prompt, navigate to your workspace and create a project folder, for example, `flask_app`. Inside this folder, initiate a virtual environment using the command `python -m venv venv`. This creates an isolated Python environment, protecting the project from dependency conflicts that could arise when working with multiple Python applications. Activating the virtual environment (`source venv/bin/activate` on Linux/macOS or `venv\Scripts\activate` on Windows) ensures that subsequent installations, including Flask, are contained within this isolated scope.

Once activated, install Flask using the command `pip install Flask`. After the installation is complete, verify the setup by creating a simple `app.py` file that prints "Hello, Flask!" when accessed through a web browser. This foundational test confirms that Flask is operational and ready for further development.

2.2 Creating a Virtual Environment

The necessity of a virtual environment in Flask development cannot be overstated, particularly in academic settings where students may be managing multiple course-related projects simultaneously. Virtual environments prevent dependency clashes and ensure consistent application behavior regardless of updates in globally installed packages. This is especially important when integrating Flask with additional libraries such as SQLAlchemy for databases or Flask-WTF for form handling.

For educational institutions, teaching the importance of virtual environments cultivates best practices early on, aligning with professional standards in software development. Furthermore, managing virtual environments using tools like `pip freeze > requirements.txt` and `pip install -r requirements.txt` enables reproducibility and collaboration—a critical competency in both academic group projects and real-world software engineering.

2.3 Folder Structure for a Flask Project

Organizing project files in a consistent and scalable structure is essential for managing code effectively as applications grow in complexity. While Flask does not enforce a strict folder structure, adopting a standardized layout facilitates code readability, maintenance, and collaborative development.

A typical Flask project might include the following directories and files: a top-level project folder containing `app.py` (the entry point of the application), a `static/` directory for CSS, JavaScript, and image files, and a `templates/` directory for HTML files. Additional folders such as `models/`, `routes/`, or `controllers/` may be introduced as the application evolves to reflect the MVC (Model-View-Controller) architecture. This modularization not only enhances maintainability

16

but also mirrors industry practices, preparing students for work in professional development teams.

For instance, when building a student record management system, models may define the database schema for students and courses, templates could render student profiles or course listings, and routes would handle HTTP requests for displaying or editing records. Structuring the project in this way allows for efficient debugging and feature scaling.

2.4 Installing Bootstrap 5.3.5 Locally

Modern web applications demand responsive, user-friendly interfaces, and integrating a front-end framework like Bootstrap addresses this need effectively. While Flask itself does not include UI components, Bootstrap provides a comprehensive toolkit of CSS and JavaScript components that simplify the design process. To install Bootstrap 5.3.5 locally, first download the distribution package from the official Bootstrap website at https://getbootstrap.com.

After downloading, extract the `bootstrap-5.3.5-dist` folder and place it inside the `static/` directory of your Flask project. This local installation ensures that the application does not rely on internet connectivity to render styles, which is particularly advantageous in educational settings where labs may have limited or controlled internet access. To link Bootstrap in your HTML templates, use the appropriate relative paths within the `<head>` tag, such as `<link rel="stylesheet" href="{{ url_for('static', filename='bootstrap-5.3.5-dist/css/bootstrap.min.css') }}">`.

To validate the integration, modify your `index.html` within the `templates/` directory to include a Bootstrap component, such as a navbar or alert box. Run the Flask app and check the browser for the correct rendering of these elements. This hands-on approach reinforces students' understanding of static file handling in Flask and front-end-back-end integration.

2.5 Introduction to Basic HTML, CSS, and Bootstrap Components

A foundational understanding of HTML and CSS is essential before effectively utilizing Bootstrap. HTML (HyperText Markup Language) structures the content of web pages, while CSS (Cascading Style Sheets) defines their appearance. Together, they form the backbone of web front-end development. Bootstrap builds upon these technologies by offering pre-designed components and responsive grid systems that significantly reduce the effort required to build visually appealing interfaces.

Students should start with simple HTML tags such as `<div>`, `<p>`, `<a>`, and `<form>`, progressing to more complex structures like tables and forms. CSS should be introduced in parallel, covering properties like color, padding, margin, and font styles. Once the basics are understood, Bootstrap components—such as buttons, cards, modals, and navigation bars—can be explored. These components are not only visually refined but also come with built-in responsiveness, ensuring optimal rendering across devices.

As a practical exercise, students might build a personal profile page using Bootstrap's card component, enriched with custom styles defined in a separate CSS file stored in the `static/` directory. By combining Flask templates with Bootstrap and custom CSS, students gain first-hand experience in developing full-stack web applications.

Conclusion

Setting up the development environment is more than a technical prerequisite—it is an initiation into the discipline of structured, maintainable, and scalable software development. Through the installation of Flask, the creation of a virtual environment, and the adoption of a clear folder structure, students are introduced to the foundational practices that govern real-world web application development. The local integration of Bootstrap 5.3.5 and an introductory exploration of HTML and CSS further enrich the learning experience, empowering learners to craft aesthetically pleasing and functionally robust user interfaces. As these foundational elements come together, they prepare the ground for building dynamic, database-driven applications in subsequent chapters.

Chapter 3: Creating Your First Flask App

Developing a foundational understanding of how Flask operates begins with constructing a simple application that demonstrates the core mechanics of the framework. This chapter introduces the essential components involved in setting up and running a basic Flask application. Through this process, students will not only become familiar with Flask's syntax and structure but also gain practical insights into how routing, templating, and static file management function cohesively in real-world web development. By the end of this chapter, students and educators will possess the competencies needed to initiate and expand Flask-based projects confidently.

3.1 Writing "Hello, World!" in Flask

Every journey in web development often begins with a "Hello, World!" program. This minimal Flask application demonstrates the simplicity and elegance of the framework. Consider the following Python code stored in a file named app.py:

```
from flask import Flask

app = Flask(__name__)

@app.route("/")
def hello():
    return "Hello, World!"
```

This application defines a single route ("/") which returns a plain text response when accessed via a web browser. The Flask object instantiation initializes the application, while the decorator @app.route("/") binds the function to the URL path. The minimalist structure illustrates Flask's core strength: its ability to deliver functionality with minimal overhead, a feature particularly useful in academic environments where learning clarity is paramount.

3.2 Understanding Routing (@app.route)

Routing is one of the most critical concepts in any web framework. In Flask, routing is managed using the `@app.route()` decorator, which maps URL endpoints to Python functions. These functions, known as *view functions*, define what content should be displayed when a user navigates to a specific path. For example:

```
@app.route("/about")
def about():
    return "This is the About page."
```

Routing empowers developers to define meaningful and organized URL structures. For educators designing instructional systems or students creating portfolio sites, a well-planned routing system facilitates seamless navigation and better user experience. Furthermore, routes can include dynamic segments, enabling content to be served based on URL parameters, as seen in this example:

```
@app.route("/user/<username>")
def show_user(username):
    return f"Hello, {username}!"
```

This use of dynamic routes enables applications to personalize content or process specific data entries, a common requirement in modern systems such as learning management platforms and inventory control apps.

3.3 Running the Flask Development Server

To run a Flask application, the development server must be started, allowing it to handle incoming HTTP requests. This is typically done by executing `flask run` in the terminal, provided the environment variable `FLASK_APP=app.py` has been correctly set. On Windows systems, this variable is set with the command `set FLASK_APP=app.py`, while on Unix-like systems, it is `export FLASK_APP=app.py`.

Once executed, Flask spins up a lightweight development server, often accessible at `http://127.0.0.1:5000/`. This server provides helpful debugging tools, such as automatic reloading and detailed error messages. These features are invaluable in academic settings where trial-and-error and incremental learning play key roles. Flask's debugger encourages students to test hypotheses and rapidly iterate, much like agile methodologies used in professional environments (Fowler, 2001).

3.4 Using Templates with Jinja2

Real-world applications rarely return plain text. Instead, they dynamically generate HTML pages that blend server-side logic with client-facing content. Flask utilizes the Jinja2 templating engine for this purpose. Jinja2 allows developers to insert Python-like expressions directly into HTML files, creating dynamic, data-driven pages.

To integrate templates, Flask requires a `templates` directory where HTML files are stored. Consider the following template saved as `templates/index.html`:

```html
<!DOCTYPE html>
<html lang="en">
<head>
    <meta charset="UTF-8">
    <title>Welcome</title>
</head>
<body>
    <h1>Hello, {{ name }}!</h1>
</body>
</html>
```

In the `app.py` file, this template can be rendered using the `render_template` function:

```
from flask import render_template

@app.route("/greet/<name>")
def greet(name):
    return render_template("index.html", name=name)
```

This example demonstrates how data passed from the server (in this case, a user's name) is embedded into the HTML using the `{{ }}` syntax. This is particularly powerful when creating dashboards or reports where data from a database needs to be presented visually to the user. The ability to separate presentation logic from application logic also reflects good software engineering practices (Gamma et al., 1994).

3.5 Static Files (CSS, JS, Images)

Modern web applications are incomplete without stylesheets, scripts, and media files. Flask handles these assets through the `static` directory. This folder contains all non-dynamic files that the browser requires to render the interface as designed. For example, Bootstrap stylesheets or custom JavaScript functions should be stored here.

To serve a CSS file, such as `style.css`, saved in the `static/css/` folder, it must be linked in the HTML as follows:

```
<link rel="stylesheet" href="{{ url_for('static',
filename='css/style.css') }}">
```

The `url_for` function ensures Flask generates the correct path to the static file, preserving portability across environments. Managing static files effectively becomes especially important when building responsive, visually engaging applications, such as e-commerce platforms or interactive educational tools.

To experiment with this, students can download Bootstrap 5.3.5, place its files inside the `static/bootstrap-5.3.5-dist/` directory, and link it in their HTML. For hands-on guidance, the Bootstrap setup tutorial on the official site provides step-by-step instructions: https://getbootstrap.com/docs/5.3/getting-started/download/. This approach not only familiarizes learners with real-world development practices but also deepens their understanding of how front-end and back-end components converge.

Conclusion

The process of creating a first Flask application introduces a spectrum of critical web development concepts—ranging from routing and dynamic content generation to managing static files and templating with Jinja2. Through this chapter, Information Technology students gain practical exposure to building modular and interactive web systems. By grounding these lessons in real-world practices and professional workflows, educators can cultivate both technical proficiency and strategic thinking in their learners. The skills acquired here will serve as the bedrock for more advanced topics such as database integration, authentication systems, and RESTful API design, which will be explored in subsequent chapters.

Chapter 4: Integrating Bootstrap 5.3.5

The integration of Bootstrap into a Flask web application is pivotal for enhancing both aesthetic quality and responsive design. Bootstrap, developed by Twitter, is one of the most widely adopted front-end frameworks in modern web development, and version 5.3.5 introduces refined design utilities and greater flexibility in component customization. This chapter delves into the structured application of Bootstrap 5.3.5 in a Flask project, ensuring that students gain proficiency in responsive layout design, effective component use, and template inheritance using Jinja2. The intention is to bridge the gap between back-end logic and front-end design by exploring real-world scenarios in which a visually engaging, responsive interface is vital— for example, in online learning portals or inventory management dashboards.

4.1 Linking Bootstrap Files from bootstrap-5.3.5-dist (Local)

In contrast to linking Bootstrap via a CDN (Content Delivery Network), local integration provides control over updates and supports offline development. This approach is particularly beneficial in academic settings or institutions with limited or regulated internet access. After downloading Bootstrap 5.3.5 from the official Bootstrap download page, extract the folder and place it in the Flask project directory under `static/bootstrap-5.3.5-dist/`.

To link the Bootstrap CSS in your HTML template, include the following code in the `<head>` section of your `base.html` file:

```
<link rel="stylesheet" href="{{ url_for('static',
filename='bootstrap-5.3.5-dist/css/bootstrap.min.css')
}}">
```

Similarly, place the JavaScript bundle just before the closing `</body>` tag:

```
<script src="{{ url_for('static', filename='bootstrap-
5.3.5-dist/js/bootstrap.bundle.min.js') }}"></script>
```

This setup ensures that your application uses Bootstrap resources directly from your project folder, reducing dependencies on external networks while providing a reliable and portable configuration.

4.2 Using Bootstrap Layout: Containers, Rows, and Columns

Bootstrap's grid system provides a highly structured method for creating responsive layouts using containers, rows, and columns. This system is based on a 12-column layout, which scales appropriately based on screen size. In a real-world scenario, such as designing a student grade dashboard, different data panels can be organized using this grid to ensure clarity across devices.

Consider the following example layout:

```
<div class="container">
    <div class="row">
        <div class="col-md-6">
            <h2>Student Performance</h2>
        </div>
        <div class="col-md-6">
            <h2>Upcoming Deadlines</h2>
        </div>
    </div>
</div>
```

Here, each `col-md-6` spans half the width of the row on medium screens and larger, stacking vertically on smaller devices. Such responsiveness is critical for educational applications where students may access systems from both desktops and smartphones.

Students must also consider layout nesting and alignment strategies to maintain design integrity. Bootstrap provides utility classes such as `d-flex`, `justify-content-center`, and `align-items-center`, which help in aligning content and achieving advanced layouts without writing custom CSS.

4.3 Using Bootstrap Components: Navbar, Buttons, and Cards

Beyond layout, Bootstrap includes a suite of reusable components that enhance user interaction and interface appeal. Among the most vital are the navbar, buttons, and cards. These components form the backbone of most modern web applications, from e-commerce sites to data portals.

A typical navbar, for example, provides navigation and branding:

```
<nav class="navbar navbar-expand-lg navbar-dark bg-
dark">
    <div class="container-fluid">
        <a class="navbar-brand" href="#">MyApp</a>
        <div class="collapse navbar-collapse">
            <ul class="navbar-nav me-auto">
                <li class="nav-item"><a class="nav-
link" href="/">Home</a></li>
                <li class="nav-item"><a class="nav-
link" href="/about">About</a></li>
            </ul>
        </div>
    </div>
</nav>
```

In professional settings, such as in municipal permit systems or university information portals, consistent navigation is essential for user retention and ease of access.

Cards are another versatile component ideal for presenting grouped data, such as student profiles or service descriptions:

```
<div class="card" style="width: 18rem;">
    <img src="{{ url_for('static',
filename='images/profile.jpg') }}" class="card-img-top"
alt="Profile">
    <div class="card-body">
        <h5 class="card-title">Jane Doe</h5>
        <p class="card-text">Computer Science Major</p>
        <a href="/profile/jane" class="btn btn-
primary">View Profile</a>
    </div>
</div>
```

The use of components not only streamlines UI development but also ensures accessibility and consistency, which are key principles in modern software engineering and usability research (Nielsen, 1995).

4.4 Creating a Base Layout (base.html) with Jinja2

In multi-page applications, it is inefficient and error-prone to repeat HTML structures such as headers, navbars, and footers across multiple templates. Flask resolves this issue using Jinja2 template inheritance. By defining a `base.html` file that contains the common layout, individual pages can extend this base and inject their content dynamically.

An example `base.html` might look like this:

```
<!DOCTYPE html>
<html lang="en">
<head>
    <meta charset="UTF-8">
```

28

```
<title>{% block title %}MyApp{% endblock %}</title>
    <link   rel="stylesheet"   href="{{  url_for('static',
filename='bootstrap-5.3.5-dist/css/bootstrap.min.css')
}}">
</head>
<body>
    {% include 'navbar.html' %}
    <div class="container mt-4">
        {% block content %}{% endblock %}
    </div>
    <script            src="{{            url_for('static',
filename='bootstrap-5.3.5-
dist/js/bootstrap.bundle.min.js') }}"></script>
</body>
</html>
```

Then, a child template such as `home.html` can extend this layout:

```
{% extends 'base.html' %}

{% block title %}Home - MyApp{% endblock %}

{% block content %}
<h1>Welcome to MyApp</h1>
<p>This platform supports academic and administrative
operations.</p>
{% endblock %}
```

This modular design mirrors best practices in professional software projects, where maintainability and scalability are prioritized. Moreover, it supports code reuse, reducing redundancy and potential for inconsistency—a concern that frequently arises in collaborative development environments.

Conclusion

Integrating Bootstrap 5.3.5 into a Flask application empowers developers to design visually coherent and mobile-friendly interfaces with minimal overhead. By understanding how to structure layouts, utilize pre-built components, and adopt templating best practices, Information Technology students are better equipped to produce professional-grade applications. These skills are particularly relevant in the development of student information systems, internal tools, and public-facing portals, where user experience and responsive design are paramount. As the foundation for future enhancements involving interactivity and database connectivity, mastering Bootstrap integration is an essential milestone in the modern web development curriculum.

Chapter 5: SQLite Database with Flask

The integration of a database into a web application marks a significant transition from static pages to dynamic, data-driven systems. Among the various database systems available, SQLite stands out due to its lightweight nature, simplicity, and zero-configuration setup. For Information Technology students and novice developers, SQLite provides an ideal entry point into understanding database interaction within a Flask framework. This chapter explores how SQLite can be used effectively with Flask to manage data, offering hands-on guidance and academic insight into structured data handling.

5.1 Introduction to SQLite

SQLite is an embedded, serverless database engine widely recognized for its minimal setup and broad application across mobile, desktop, and web platforms. Unlike client-server databases such as MySQL or PostgreSQL, SQLite writes directly to a local file, making it ideal for prototyping, educational applications, and small-scale deployments. Its popularity is reflected in its usage by prominent applications such as Mozilla Firefox and Android OS (Owens, 2010). For Flask developers, the advantage lies in seamless integration and minimal overhead, which accelerates learning and development processes without the need to configure a separate database server.

In the context of a Flask web application, SQLite is commonly used for systems such as student feedback forms, event registration portals, and library search platforms. These use cases do not demand high concurrency or complex transaction management, allowing developers to focus on core logic and user experience.

5.2 Creating a Database File

To begin working with SQLite in a Flask app, the first step is to create a database file. This file acts as a container for tables and records, and is usually stored in a dedicated `instance` or `data` folder for separation of concerns. In practice, Flask provides flexibility in handling file paths through configuration variables.

Consider the following initialization process:

```
import sqlite3

connection = sqlite3.connect('instance/app.db')
cursor = connection.cursor()
```

Here, `app.db` is the SQLite database file that will hold your data. The file is created automatically if it does not already exist. For a more persistent and scalable approach, Flask developers typically wrap this logic inside a helper function or context manager, allowing the database connection to be reused across routes without redundancy.

5.3 Using Flask's sqlite3 Module

Flask includes built-in support for SQLite through the `sqlite3` module in Python's standard library. While developers may later explore ORM (Object-Relational Mapping) tools like SQLAlchemy, direct use of `sqlite3` is beneficial for students to understand raw SQL execution and cursor-based interactions.

A practical method to encapsulate database access is through a function that returns a connection tied to the Flask application context:

```
from flask import g

def get_db():
    if 'db' not in g:
        g.db = sqlite3.connect('instance/app.db')
```

```
    g.db.row_factory = sqlite3.Row
return g.db
```

This approach allows persistent connections during a request, enabling multiple queries without reopening the database. The `row_factory` setting converts query results into dictionaries, improving readability and access via column names rather than indices.

5.4 Creating Tables Using SQL

To define the structure of your data, SQL (Structured Query Language) is used to create tables. Tables are composed of columns with specific data types and constraints. For instance, a basic student table may include columns for `id`, `name`, `email`, and `course`.

The SQL command for this table might appear as follows:

```
CREATE TABLE IF NOT EXISTS students (
    id INTEGER PRIMARY KEY AUTOINCREMENT,
    name TEXT NOT NULL,
    email TEXT UNIQUE NOT NULL,
    course TEXT NOT NULL
);
```

To execute this command in a Flask app, you can include the following function:

```
def init_db():
    db = get_db()
    with open('schema.sql') as f:
        db.executescript(f.read())
```

This function reads from a schema file and initializes the database with the required tables. Real-world applications, such as class attendance systems or digital grading portals, rely on such schema design to ensure data integrity and avoid duplication.

5.5 Inserting and Retrieving Data

Once tables are in place, the application must support data manipulation operations such as INSERT, SELECT, UPDATE, and DELETE. Inserting data typically follows a user form submission, such as a student filling out their details. This data is captured in a route using Flask's `request` object and stored using parameterized queries to avoid SQL injection.

Example of inserting a student:

```
@app.route('/add_student', methods=['POST'])
def add_student():
    name = request.form['name']
    email = request.form['email']
    course = request.form['course']
    db = get_db()
    db.execute('INSERT   INTO   students   (name,   email,
course) VALUES (?, ?, ?)',
                (name, email, course))
    db.commit()
    return redirect('/')
```

Retrieving data is often necessary for displaying records in templates. Using a SELECT query, the application fetches records and passes them to the view:

```
@app.route('/students')
def show_students():
    db = get_db()
    students   =   db.execute('SELECT   *   FROM
students').fetchall()
    return   render_template('students.html',
students=students)
```

The `students.html` template then iterates over the `students` list using Jinja2 to generate a table. This pattern is prevalent in administrative dashboards where records must be displayed dynamically with real-time data.

Conclusion

The use of SQLite in Flask applications bridges theoretical database design with practical implementation. For Information Technology students, this hands-on experience reinforces concepts of data modeling, query formulation, and software modularity. Moreover, it introduces essential development practices such as code reusability, security through query parameterization, and separation of logic from presentation. These principles mirror industry expectations and align with academic goals, ensuring that learners are well-equipped to transition from classroom projects to real-world systems development. As projects grow, students may further expand their skills by integrating more robust database systems or adopting ORM tools, building on the foundational understanding acquired through SQLite.

Chapter 6: Building a Dynamic Web Application

Developing a dynamic web application requires an understanding of both front-end user interaction and back-end data processing. This chapter examines how to build a user-responsive Flask application by collecting, validating, and displaying user data through HTML forms and database interaction. Information Technology students and educators often focus on these foundational concepts to bridge static content delivery with real-time user engagement, forming the cornerstone of any interactive system, from simple blogs to comprehensive management systems.

6.1 Accepting User Input with HTML Forms

User input is central to any dynamic application. Whether it involves login credentials, registration forms, survey submissions, or product search queries, HTML forms provide the structure through which users can send data to a web server. In Flask, forms are typically integrated into Jinja2 templates using standard HTML syntax.

For instance, consider a simple feedback form in `feedback.html`:

```
<form action="/submit_feedback" method="POST">
  <label for="name">Name:</label>
  <input type="text" name="name" required>

  <label for="feedback">Feedback:</label>
  <textarea name="feedback" required></textarea>

  <button type="submit">Submit</button>
</form>
```

This form sends user input to the /submit_feedback route using the POST method, ensuring that data is not exposed in the URL. In real-world scenarios, such as e-learning platforms or online customer service portals, forms like this are critical for capturing structured user feedback that can be stored and analyzed.

6.2 Handling Form Data in Flask (`request.form`)

Once a form is submitted, Flask provides a simple and secure way to access the input using the `request.form` dictionary. This feature allows developers to process and store data while maintaining full control over validation and flow control.

The following route demonstrates how to handle the submitted form data:

```
from flask import request, redirect, url_for,
render_template

@app.route('/submit_feedback', methods=['POST'])
def submit_feedback():
    name = request.form['name']
    feedback = request.form['feedback']
    db = get_db()
    db.execute('INSERT INTO feedbacks (name, feedback)
VALUES (?, ?)', (name, feedback))
    db.commit()
    return redirect(url_for('thank_you'))
```

Here, data is securely retrieved from the request object and written to a database. This pattern aligns with typical real-world use cases such as saving customer testimonials or student evaluations, where user-generated content must be stored for analysis or future reference.

6.3 Validating Form Input

Form validation is critical to ensuring data quality, security, and user experience. Although HTML5 provides some level of client-side validation through attributes like `required` and `type`, robust systems must implement server-side validation to avoid malformed or malicious data.

For example, before inserting into the database, the application should validate that the user has provided non-empty and reasonable-length input:

```
@app.route('/submit_feedback', methods=['POST'])
def submit_feedback():
    name = request.form['name'].strip()
    feedback = request.form['feedback'].strip()

    if not name or not feedback:
        error = "All fields are required."
        return render_template('feedback.html',
error=error)

    db = get_db()
    db.execute('INSERT INTO feedbacks (name, feedback)
VALUES (?, ?)', (name, feedback))
    db.commit()
    return redirect(url_for('thank_you'))
```

Validation not only prevents empty submissions but also guards against SQL injection, spam, and inconsistent records. This is especially important in education management systems or government platforms where data integrity and security are paramount.

6.4 Displaying Database Records Dynamically in HTML

After collecting and storing data, the next step is to display it in a user-friendly format. Dynamic rendering allows the content of a page to be populated with real-time data from the database. Using Flask's `render_template` function in combination with Jinja2, developers can loop through query results and embed them into structured HTML.

Consider this example of displaying feedbacks from a SQLite database:

```
@app.route('/feedbacks')
def feedbacks():
    db = get_db()
    entries = db.execute('SELECT name, feedback FROM
feedbacks').fetchall()
    return render_template('display_feedbacks.html',
entries=entries)
```

And in the corresponding template `display_feedbacks.html`:

```
<h2>User Feedback</h2>
{% for entry in entries %}
  <div class="card my-3">
    <div class="card-body">
      <h5 class="card-title">{{ entry['name'] }}</h5>
      <p class="card-text">{{ entry['feedback'] }}</p>
    </div>
  </div>
{% endfor %}
```

Using Bootstrap classes, developers can create an aesthetically pleasing and responsive layout. This pattern is common in student project portals, product review sites, and administrative dashboards, where real-time updates and presentation of user-submitted data enhance transparency and usability.

Conclusion

Building dynamic web applications with Flask introduces learners to the full lifecycle of data interaction—from form creation and input collection to validation and dynamic display. By mastering these concepts, Information Technology students gain practical experience that translates into real-world systems development. These foundational skills empower students to build more advanced features such as user authentication, AJAX-based interactivity, and RESTful APIs. Moreover, by incorporating best practices in input handling and data rendering, developers ensure their applications are not only functional but also secure, scalable, and user-friendly. This integration of theory and practice solidifies Flask's role as a powerful yet accessible tool for teaching and implementing dynamic web development.

Chapter 7: CRUD Functionality with SQLite

Modern web applications often revolve around CRUD functionality—Create, Read, Update, and Delete—as the foundational operations for managing data. Whether it's a content management system, a student records portal, or a customer support database, these operations provide users with the ability to manipulate and interact with stored information. This chapter delves into implementing CRUD using Flask and SQLite, guiding learners through real-world web development practices with a focus on academic rigor and application reliability.

7.1 Create: Inserting New Records

In any data-driven application, inserting new records marks the entry point of data lifecycle management. Flask facilitates this operation by handling user input via HTML forms and storing it securely using SQLite commands. Consider an application that manages a student directory. A form collects input such as the student's name, email, and course. Once submitted, the backend uses parameterized SQL queries to insert the new data into the database, thereby minimizing the risk of SQL injection.

The route might look like this:

```
@app.route('/add', methods=['GET', 'POST'])
def add_student():
    if request.method == 'POST':
        name = request.form['name']
        email = request.form['email']
        course = request.form['course']
        db = get_db()
```

```
      db.execute('INSERT INTO students (name, email,
course) VALUES (?, ?, ?)', (name, email, course))
      db.commit()
      return redirect(url_for('index'))
   return render_template('add_student.html')
```

Real-world applications such as enrollment systems and contact management platforms use similar logic to store and organize new entries. The emphasis on form validation and secure database operations ensures robust functionality.

7.2 Read: Displaying Data in Tables or Cards

Displaying stored data enables users to visualize and verify the content they or others have submitted. Flask integrates seamlessly with Jinja2 to render this data dynamically within structured HTML templates. Depending on the application's design, data can be displayed in tabular form for clarity or using Bootstrap cards for a modern aesthetic.

In an academic records system, the display route may be structured as follows:

```
@app.route('/')
def index():
    db = get_db()
    students = db.execute('SELECT id, name, email,
course FROM students').fetchall()
    return render_template('index.html',
students=students)
```

The corresponding HTML template might use Bootstrap's table structure:

```
<table class="table table-bordered">
  <thead>
```

```
<tr><th>Name</th><th>Email</th><th>Course</th><th>Actio
ns</th></tr>
  </thead>
  <tbody>
    {% for student in students %}
    <tr>
      <td>{{ student['name'] }}</td>
      <td>{{ student['email'] }}</td>
      <td>{{ student['course'] }}</td>
      <td>
        <a href="{{ url_for('edit_student',
id=student['id']) }}" class="btn btn-sm btn-
warning">Edit</a>
        <a href="{{ url_for('delete_student',
id=student['id']) }}" class="btn btn-sm btn-
danger">Delete</a>
      </td>
    </tr>
    {% endfor %}
  </tbody>
</table>
```

This approach is widely used in dashboards, data monitoring systems, and educational portals where administrators need instant visibility into the stored data.

7.3 Update: Editing Existing Records

Updating records introduces users to more complex interactions. Typically, a user selects an item to edit, is redirected to a pre-filled form, makes necessary changes, and submits the form to overwrite the existing database entry. Flask routes handle both displaying the form and processing the updated data.

```
@app.route('/edit/<int:id>', methods=['GET', 'POST'])
def edit_student(id):
    db = get_db()
    if request.method == 'POST':
        name = request.form['name']
```

```
        email = request.form['email']
        course = request.form['course']
        db.execute('UPDATE students SET name = ?, email
= ?, course = ? WHERE id = ?', (name, email, course,
id))
        db.commit()
        return redirect(url_for('index'))
    student = db.execute('SELECT * FROM students WHERE
id = ?', (id,)).fetchone()
    return render_template('edit_student.html',
student=student)
```

In practice, this model supports various platforms including HR systems, inventory management tools, and profile editing modules. The use of parameterized queries ensures that even during updates, data integrity and security remain uncompromised.

7.4 Delete: Removing Records

Deleting records must be handled with caution to prevent accidental data loss. While the interface typically provides a "Delete" button, backend logic confirms the record's existence and securely removes it. Additionally, developers often implement confirmation prompts in the frontend to reduce errors.

```
@app.route('/delete/<int:id>', methods=['GET'])
def delete_student(id):
    db = get_db()
    db.execute('DELETE FROM students WHERE id = ?',
(id,))
    db.commit()
    return redirect(url_for('index'))
```

This pattern is common in content moderation dashboards, e-commerce platforms (removing outdated products), and academic systems where incorrect records need to be purged. Depending on requirements, soft deletes (marking records as inactive) may also be considered.

7.5 Creating Dynamic Routes (`/edit/<id>`)

Dynamic routing is pivotal for enabling user-specific interactions with content. In Flask, routes such as `/edit/<id>` or `/profile/<username>` help bind URL patterns to database entries. These routes improve user experience by allowing deep linking and personalized content access.

The use of `<int:id>` ensures Flask interprets the parameter as an integer, improving route matching accuracy and data lookup efficiency. This mechanism is particularly useful in e-commerce websites (e.g., `/product/342`), learning platforms (`/course/21`), and news portals (`/article/145`), where dynamic content must be fetched and rendered based on unique identifiers.

Conclusion

Implementing CRUD functionality using Flask and SQLite provides a solid foundation for developing responsive, user-centric applications. These core operations not only enable data management but also cultivate essential skills in database manipulation, input handling, and dynamic UI development. The hands-on integration of these features prepares students for real-world development environments, including SaaS platforms, enterprise dashboards, and digital libraries. Moreover, by following secure coding practices and user-friendly design principles, developers ensure their applications are scalable, reliable, and accessible—hallmarks of effective information systems development.

Chapter 8: Organizing Your Flask Application

In the early stages of developing Flask applications, it's common to build everything in a single file such as `app.py`. While this approach may suffice for small projects or quick prototypes, it becomes increasingly difficult to manage and scale as the application grows. To ensure maintainability, readability, and scalability, developers are encouraged to modularize their codebase. This chapter explores the significance of organizing Flask applications using Blueprints, separating functionalities into distinct files, and adopting best practices for folder structures. It also explains the pivotal role of the `__init__.py` file in initializing modular applications.

8.1 Using Blueprints to Modularize Your App

Flask Blueprints are a powerful feature that allows developers to split large applications into smaller, logically grouped components. Each Blueprint represents a subset of the application, encapsulating its routes, templates, and static files. This is especially beneficial in real-world scenarios such as developing a university management system where different modules—like students, faculty, courses, and administration—can be isolated into individual Blueprints.

Consider an academic portal where students and faculty need separate dashboards. Using Blueprints, developers can create a `student` Blueprint and a `faculty` Blueprint, each with its own routing and templates. Here's an example of creating a student Blueprint:

```
# student/routes.py
from flask import Blueprint, render_template
```

```
student_bp = Blueprint('student', __name__,
url_prefix='/student')

@student_bp.route('/dashboard')
def dashboard():
    return render_template('student/dashboard.html')
```

This Blueprint is then registered in the main application inside the `__init__.py` file, ensuring modular architecture and promoting code reuse across different parts of the app.

8.2 Creating Separate Files for Routes, Forms, and Models

A core tenet of software engineering is the separation of concerns. For Flask applications, this principle can be realized by dividing code into files according to functionality—routes handle logic, forms manage user input, and models interface with the database. This division not only improves clarity but also streamlines collaborative development in teams.

For example, in a job application system, separate Python files might be structured as:

- `routes.py` — Contains endpoints such as `/apply`, `/status`, and `/interview`.
- `forms.py` — Uses Flask-WTF to define and validate application forms.
- `models.py` — Contains SQLAlchemy or raw SQL definitions of applicants, recruiters, and job postings.

Such modularization ensures that if a developer is tasked with changing the form validation logic, they do not need to sift through unrelated route or model definitions. Moreover, it fosters testability and scalability—two vital aspects in production-ready systems.

8.3 Best Practices for App Folder Structure

As Flask applications expand, adhering to a consistent and well-documented folder structure becomes imperative. A recommended structure for medium to large Flask applications is as follows:

```
my_flask_app/
|
├── app/
|    ├── __init__.py
|    ├── routes/
|    |    ├── __init__.py
|    |    └── student_routes.py
|    |    └── faculty_routes.py
|    ├── models/
|    |    ├── __init__.py
|    |    └── student_model.py
|    ├── forms/
|    |    ├── __init__.py
|    |    └── registration_form.py
|    ├── templates/
|    |    └── base.html
|    └── static/
|         ├── css/
|         └── js/
|
├── config.py
├── run.py
└── requirements.txt
```

This layout promotes clean code and intuitive navigation, especially when multiple developers are contributing to the same codebase. It aligns well with software development practices taught in IT education, emphasizing structure and documentation for easier onboarding and debugging.

8.4 Understanding `__init__.py`

In Python, the `__init__.py` file is traditionally used to mark a directory as a package. In the context of Flask, it also plays a crucial role in initializing the application instance and binding Blueprints and extensions. This file becomes the entry point for assembling the modular components of the app.

Consider the following implementation of `app/__init__.py`:

```
from flask import Flask

def create_app():
    app = Flask(__name__)
    app.config['SECRET_KEY'] = 'your_secret_key'

    from app.routes.student_routes import student_bp
    from app.routes.faculty_routes import faculty_bp

    app.register_blueprint(student_bp)
    app.register_blueprint(faculty_bp)

    return app
```

This pattern, known as the application factory pattern, is considered a best practice in Flask development. It allows multiple configurations (e.g., development, testing, production) and supports deferred initialization of extensions and Blueprints. In professional environments, such as enterprise platforms and cloud-based services, this flexibility is crucial for deploying robust applications.

Conclusion

Organizing a Flask application effectively is more than a matter of aesthetics—it is a fundamental practice that influences maintainability, scalability, and developer productivity. Through Blueprints, developers can modularize functionality, making it easier to manage and extend. By separating files according to functionality—routes, forms, models—teams can work concurrently without overlap or confusion. A standardized folder structure coupled with a well-configured `__init__.py` ensures that even complex systems remain comprehensible and adaptable. These organizational strategies are not merely theoretical; they are observed in real-world platforms from learning management systems to government portals. As Information Technology students and educators delve deeper into Flask, understanding and implementing these practices will serve as a cornerstone for building efficient and professional-grade web applications.

Chapter 9: User Authentication (Optional, Intermediate)

In the development of dynamic web applications, particularly those involving personalized user interactions such as dashboards, form submissions, or data privacy, implementing user authentication is essential. Authentication ensures that only registered and verified users gain access to protected resources. In Flask, building a secure and scalable login and registration system involves several key components, including password hashing, session management, and user feedback mechanisms. This chapter explores these elements through real-world applications and hands-on guidance to support both students and educators in mastering secure web development.

9.1 Creating a Login and Registration System

To understand the necessity of a login system, consider an e-learning platform where students can access personalized course materials and progress reports. Without authentication, the system would be vulnerable to unauthorized access, potentially compromising sensitive academic data. Flask allows the development of such systems using its built-in functionality and additional modules like `Flask-WTF` and `Flask-Login`.

Start by creating two forms: one for user registration and another for login. These forms collect essential information such as username, email, and password. To define the forms securely, Flask-WTF (a wrapper around WTForms) can be used to validate user input. A sample registration form would include fields with validators to prevent missing data and ensure email format correctness. These forms should be linked to SQLite tables where user data is stored, making them persistent and queryable.

A practical example to implement this functionality can be found at Real Python's Flask Login System Tutorial, which demonstrates a step-by-step approach to building secure login and registration routes using blueprints.

9.2 Password Hashing with Werkzeug

Security is paramount in any authentication system. Plain-text passwords pose a severe risk if the database is ever compromised. Flask leverages the `Werkzeug` library to implement password hashing, which converts readable passwords into irreversible, encrypted strings before storage.

When a user registers, their password should be passed through `generate_password_hash()` from `werkzeug.security`. Later, during login, `check_password_hash()` verifies the input against the stored hash. This method ensures passwords are never stored in a vulnerable format. For example:

```
from werkzeug.security import generate_password_hash,
check_password_hash

hashed_pw = generate_password_hash('student123')
is_valid = check_password_hash(hashed_pw, 'student123')
```

This process mirrors best practices in enterprise systems such as online banking platforms and government portals, where password encryption is mandated by compliance standards like GDPR and HIPAA. Teaching students about hashing introduces them to fundamental cybersecurity principles and mitigates risks in real-world deployments.

9.3 Using Flask Session for Login State

Once a user is authenticated, the system must recognize and retain the user's state throughout the session. Flask provides a built-in `session` object that stores user-specific data using secure cookies. This object can be used to store variables like `user_id` or `username`, which then become accessible across different views of the application.

Consider a scenario where a logged-in user is redirected to their dashboard. Flask checks the session variable to confirm authentication before granting access. If the session lacks the proper credentials, the user is redirected to the login page. Here is an example implementation:

```python
from flask import session, redirect, url_for

@app.route('/dashboard')
def dashboard():
    if 'user_id' nct in session:
        return redirect(url_for('login'))
    return render_template('dashboard.html')
```

Using sessions in this way is crucial in preventing unauthorized access to protected routes and data. It also allows developers to implement logout functionality easily by clearing the session using `session.clear()`.

9.4 Flash Messages for User Feedback

Effective user communication enhances usability and encourages proper interaction with the application. Flask's `flash()` method allows developers to send short messages to users after critical actions, such as successful registration, incorrect login attempts, or access denials.

Imagine an HR recruitment portal where applicants are required to log in before uploading resumes. If a login fails due to incorrect credentials, a flash message can inform the user immediately without revealing sensitive information. Similarly, upon successful logout, a message like "You have been logged out" confirms the action and provides clarity.

Here's how to use flash messages in a template:

```
from flask import flash, get_flashed_messages

@app.route('/login', methods=['POST'])
def login():
    # ...authentication logic
    if login_successful:
        flash('Welcome back!')
    else:
        flash('Invalid username or password.')
```

In your base.html, include a snippet to render these messages:

```
{% with messages = get_flashed_messages() %}
  {% if messages %}
    <ul class="flashes">
    {% for message in messages %}
      <li>{{ message }}</li>
    {% endfor %}
    </ul>
  {% endif %}
{% endwith %}
```

These feedback mechanisms improve user experience and align with principles of human-computer interaction (HCI), which emphasize visibility of system status and clear communication.

Conclusion

Implementing user authentication is not merely a feature—it is a cornerstone of modern web applications. Through Flask's flexible architecture, developers can create secure login and registration systems, apply best practices such as password hashing, and ensure a smooth user experience with sessions and flash messages. By following the structured steps outlined in this chapter, students and practitioners gain the practical skills and theoretical understanding necessary for real-world application development. As web security continues to be a critical concern globally, fluency in authentication systems empowers future developers to build safer and more trustworthy platforms.

Chapter 10: Deploying Your Flask App

Deployment is one of the most critical stages in the software development lifecycle. It transitions an application from the local development environment to a live, production environment where it becomes accessible to users. Flask, being a lightweight and flexible web framework, allows developers to deploy applications in various environments, ranging from simple platforms like PythonAnywhere to complex configurations using Linux servers with Nginx and Gunicorn. This chapter will guide you through preparing your Flask application for production, setting up deployment configurations, using different hosting platforms, and managing sensitive information like environment variables and database backups.

10.1 Preparing for Production

Before deploying your Flask app, it is essential to optimize it for production environments. Development settings, such as the debug mode, should be turned off to enhance security and performance. In the development environment, Flask automatically reloads the application when changes are made. However, in production, it is critical to ensure that the app runs efficiently without unnecessary overhead. This requires the use of a production-ready server such as Gunicorn, which is capable of handling multiple requests concurrently and can scale with increasing traffic.

Flask's built-in server is not suited for production because it does not handle multiple concurrent requests efficiently. Therefore, preparing your app for production involves configuring it to run on a WSGI (Web Server Gateway Interface) server like Gunicorn, which provides better concurrency and performance. Additionally, the production environment needs proper logging configurations, error handling mechanisms, and security measures, such as the use of HTTPS. Flask applications should also implement middleware to protect against attacks like SQL injection, cross-site scripting (XSS), and cross-site request forgery (CSRF).

10.2 Using Gunicorn and Nginx (for Linux)

A common production setup for Flask applications is the combination of Gunicorn and Nginx. Gunicorn acts as the WSGI server that handles HTTP requests, while Nginx serves as the reverse proxy server that routes requests to Gunicorn and handles static files.

On a Linux server, the deployment typically begins with installing Gunicorn:

```
pip install gunicorn
```

Next, you will run your Flask application with Gunicorn:

```
gunicorn --workers 3 myapp:app
```

The `--workers` flag specifies the number of worker processes Gunicorn should use, which depends on the hardware and expected traffic. Gunicorn is configured to serve the application, while Nginx, which sits in front of Gunicorn, routes requests to it and serves static content efficiently. Here, Nginx can manage SSL certificates for HTTPS, provide load balancing, and handle other network-level concerns.

To configure Nginx, a basic server block in the Nginx configuration file might look like this:

```
server {
    listen 80;
    server_name mydomain.com;
```

```
location / {
    proxy_pass http://127.0.0.1:8000;
    proxy_set_header Host $host;
    proxy_set_header X-Real-IP $remote_addr;
    proxy_set_header X-Forwarded-For
$proxy_add_x_forwarded_for;
    proxy_set_header X-Forwarded-Proto $scheme;
}

location /static {
    alias /path/to/your/static/directory;
}
}
```

This configuration directs traffic to the Gunicorn server while serving static assets (CSS, images, JavaScript) directly via Nginx. By configuring Nginx to handle SSL, such as using Let's Encrypt, you can also ensure secure communication over HTTPS.

10.3 Hosting Options: PythonAnywhere, Heroku, or Vercel

For those who want an easier, platform-as-a-service (PaaS) solution, several hosting platforms offer simple deployment setups for Flask applications. Platforms like **Heroku**, **PythonAnywhere**, and **Vercel** simplify the deployment process, abstracting away much of the server management involved in traditional deployment.

- **Heroku**: This is one of the most popular cloud platforms for beginners and advanced developers alike. It simplifies Flask deployment using Git-based workflows. Developers push their app to Heroku, where it is automatically built and deployed. Heroku supports many add-ons, such as databases (e.g., PostgreSQL, Redis) and caching systems, making it easy to scale applications without the need for managing infrastructure. The deployment process involves creating a

`Procfile` that tells Heroku how to run the application and pushing it using Git commands:

```
git push heroku master
```

A detailed tutorial on Heroku deployment can be found at Flask on Heroku Documentation.

- **PythonAnywhere**: This platform allows users to deploy Flask applications directly from a browser interface. PythonAnywhere is an excellent option for beginners due to its simplicity and beginner-friendly pricing model. Users can deploy apps by creating a new web app in PythonAnywhere and linking it to a GitHub repository or uploading the code directly.
- **Vercel**: Vercel is another platform that focuses on serverless deployment. While it is more commonly used for static sites, it can deploy Flask apps through serverless functions, which provide automatic scaling and zero-maintenance hosting. This makes it an ideal solution for apps with low to medium traffic.

10.4 Environment Variables and Secrets

When deploying a Flask app, it's essential to manage sensitive information, such as database credentials, API keys, and secret tokens, securely. Storing such information directly in the code is unsafe and exposes the application to vulnerabilities. Instead, environment variables provide a secure mechanism for storing secrets and configuration settings.

On Linux, you can set environment variables in the terminal:

```
export FLASK_APP=myapp.py
export FLASK_ENV=production
```

You can also use a `.env` file, which can be read by the application with the help of the `python-dotenv` library. This approach allows you to keep environment-specific configurations separate from your codebase.

For example, a `.env` file might look like this:

```
FLASK_APP=myapp.py
SECRET_KEY=mysecretkey
DATABASE_URL=sqlite:///mydatabase.db
```

Flask can automatically load these variables when the application starts, ensuring that sensitive data is never hardcoded into the codebase. Additionally, services like Heroku, PythonAnywhere, and Vercel allow you to set environment variables through their web interfaces, further simplifying the process.

10.5 Backup and Restore SQLite Database

In production environments, database integrity and availability are critical. For Flask applications using SQLite, regular backups are necessary to prevent data loss in case of corruption or server failure. Since SQLite stores the entire database as a single file, backing it up is as simple as copying the database file to a secure location.

However, as SQLite is not typically used in high-traffic production systems (where databases like PostgreSQL or MySQL are preferred), it is essential to understand the limitations of SQLite in production environments. For applications with more significant data and concurrent access, consider transitioning to a more robust relational database system.

To back up an SQLite database, you can use simple file copy commands in the terminal:

```
cp mydatabase.db /path/to/backup/mydatabase_backup.db
```

Restoring the database is as simple as copying the backup file back to its original location. For more complex database management, integrating SQLite with a cloud-based storage system like Amazon S3 or Google Cloud Storage may provide additional redundancy and scalability.

Conclusion

Deploying a Flask application is a multifaceted process that involves preparing the app for production, choosing the right hosting solution, securing sensitive data, and ensuring the system remains reliable and scalable. By leveraging technologies like Gunicorn and Nginx on Linux or using simpler PaaS platforms like Heroku or PythonAnywhere, developers can find solutions suited to their application needs. Proper handling of environment variables and securing database backups are crucial for maintaining the integrity and security of the deployed application. As the web continues to evolve, understanding deployment practices ensures that Flask applications can be efficiently transitioned to production and reliably serve users.

Chapter 11: Adding More Features (Optional)

As your Flask application evolves, the need for advanced features that enhance user experience and functionality becomes inevitable. Flask's minimalistic approach allows developers to scale their applications by integrating additional functionalities, such as asynchronous data loading with AJAX, visualizing data with charts, managing file uploads, and handling pagination and filtering efficiently. These features not only improve the user interface but also enhance the backend efficiency of your application. This chapter will explore these advanced capabilities, offering practical solutions and real-world applications.

11.1 AJAX and Fetch API Integration

In modern web applications, user experience often demands that content is dynamically updated without requiring a full page reload. This is where AJAX (Asynchronous JavaScript and XML) comes in. AJAX enables web pages to send and receive data asynchronously, making it possible to update parts of a page without refreshing the whole document. Flask, being a lightweight framework, integrates well with AJAX, allowing developers to build dynamic, real-time applications.

The Fetch API, a modern JavaScript method, has largely replaced traditional AJAX requests, providing a more powerful and flexible way to make asynchronous HTTP requests. In a real-world scenario, consider an application where users need to view updated content without waiting for a full page reload. A common example would be a product listing page where the user can filter products based on categories, and the page dynamically updates based on the selected filters.

To implement this, you can use Flask to handle requests, while the front end uses JavaScript's Fetch API to fetch new data. Below is a simplified implementation:

```
fetch('/get_data')
  .then(response => response.json())
  .then(data => {
    // Update DOM elements with new data
    document.getElementById('product-list').innerHTML =
data.html;
  });
```

On the Flask side, you would handle the route and return the updated data:

```
@app.route('/get_data')
def get_data():
    products = get_products_from_database()  # Fetch
data from your database
    return jsonify({'html':
render_template('product_list.html',
products=products)})
```

This approach improves user experience by reducing server load and increasing the responsiveness of the application, which is especially beneficial for applications with large datasets or frequent updates.

11.2 Charts with Chart.js or Bootstrap Tables

Data visualization is an essential aspect of modern web applications. Whether you're building an analytics dashboard or displaying reports, using charts can present complex data in an easily digestible format. Chart.js is a versatile and lightweight JavaScript library that allows you to render interactive charts in a web page.

Integrating Chart.js into a Flask application is straightforward. Consider a real-world scenario where you are building a dashboard that visualizes user activity over time. To display a simple line chart of user sign-ups per month, you would fetch the data from the Flask backend and pass it to the frontend where Chart.js will render the chart.

Here's a simple example of how you could implement this:

In Flask:

```
@app.route('/chart_data')
def chart_data():
    data = get_monthly_signups()  # Fetch data from
your database
    return jsonify(data)
```

In JavaScript, you could fetch this data and render a Chart.js chart:

```
fetch('/chart_data')
  .then(response => response.json())
  .then(data => {
    new Chart(document.getElementById("signup-chart"),
{
      type: 'line',
      data: {
        labels: data.labels,  // Array of months
        datasets: [{
          label: 'Monthly Signups',
          data: data.values,  // Array of user counts
        }]
      }
    });
  });
```

For applications requiring tables, Bootstrap provides responsive table components that can be enhanced with dynamic features like sorting and filtering. A common use case might be displaying a list of users, where users can search, sort, and filter the data displayed. Flask integrates well with these features by providing the backend API to fetch the data and update the table on the frontend.

11.3 File Uploads and Downloads

File uploads are a common requirement in web applications. Whether it's users uploading images, documents, or other types of files, handling file uploads securely and efficiently is crucial. Flask provides the `request` object to handle file uploads, while HTML forms allow users to select and send files.

A practical example is building a file-sharing platform where users can upload and download documents. To allow file uploads, the form in the HTML template must include `enctype="multipart/form-data"` to handle file submissions. Here's a basic example:

```
<form action="/upload" method="POST"
enctype="multipart/form-data">
  <input type="file" name="file" />
  <input type="submit" value="Upload" />
</form>
```

In Flask, the route to handle the file upload looks like this:

```
@app.route('/upload', methods=['POST'])
def upload_file():
    file = request.files['file']
    if file:
        filepath =
os.path.join(app.config['UPLOAD_FOLDER'],
file.filename)
        file.save(filepath)
        return redirect(url_for('index'))
```

For file downloads, you can simply provide a link or button to the user, and Flask will handle the response, sending the file to the browser:

```
@app.route('/download/<filename>')
```

```
def download_file(filename):
    return
send_from_directory(app.config['UPLOAD_FOLDER'],
filename)
```

11.4 Pagination and Filtering

Pagination and filtering are essential features for any application that handles large sets of data. They allow users to navigate through data without overwhelming them with excessive information. For instance, if your application lists blog posts, products, or customer orders, implementing pagination ensures that the data is presented in manageable chunks.

Flask's interaction with pagination typically involves querying a database for a limited set of records. You can use SQLAlchemy's built-in pagination methods to fetch a specific range of data. Here's a simple example of implementing pagination in a Flask app:

```
@app.route('/products')
def products():
    page = request.args.get('page', 1, type=int)
    products = Product.query.paginate(page,
per_page=10)
    return render_template('products.html',
products=products)
```

On the front end, you can create links for navigating through pages:

```
{% for product in products.items %}
  <p>{{ product.name }}</p>
{% endfor %}

<div>
  <a href="{{ url_for('products',
page=products.prev_num) }}">Previous</a>
  <a href="{{ url_for('products',
page=products.next_num) }}">Next</a>
</div>
```

Filtering is another useful feature, enabling users to search and narrow down results based on certain criteria. This can be achieved using query parameters in the URL or through JavaScript, allowing the backend to filter results based on the user's input.

11.5 Using Flask-WTF for Form Handling

Forms are an integral part of web applications, and Flask-WTF simplifies form handling in Flask by integrating with WTForms, which provides easy form validation and CSRF protection. Flask-WTF also allows developers to define forms as Python classes, making it easier to manage form fields and validations.

Consider a user registration form where you need to validate the email and password. Flask-WTF simplifies this by providing built-in field types and validators. Here's an example of how you would use Flask-WTF for a registration form:

In Python:

```
from flask_wtf import FlaskForm
from wtforms import StringField, PasswordField
from wtforms.validators import DataRequired, Email,
Length

class RegistrationForm(FlaskForm):
    email = StringField('Email',
validators=[DataRequired(), Email()])
    password = PasswordField('Password',
validators=[DataRequired(), Length(min=6)])
```

In the template, you render the form fields:

```
<form method="POST" action="/register">
  {{ form.hidden_tag() }}
  <div>{{ form.email.label }} {{ form.email() }}</div>
  <div>{{ form.password.label }} {{ form.password()
}}</div>
```

```
<button type="submit">Register</button>
</form>
```

This ensures that the form is protected against CSRF attacks and performs server-side validation, making form handling in Flask both secure and efficient.

Conclusion

Adding advanced features such as AJAX integration, data visualization, file uploads, pagination, and form handling can significantly enhance the functionality and user experience of a Flask application. By integrating technologies like Chart.js, Flask-WTF, and using Flask's robust handling for file operations and data queries, developers can build dynamic, interactive web applications that meet the needs of modern users. These features, while optional, are crucial in developing real-world applications that scale effectively and provide a polished user experience.

Chapter 12: Final Project and Review

As the culmination of this learning journey, your final project presents an invaluable opportunity to apply the concepts and skills you've developed throughout this course. In this chapter, we will guide you through planning, implementing, and refining a mini-project using Flask. A well-executed final project not only demonstrates your proficiency with Flask but also provides a tangible portfolio piece that showcases your development abilities. Whether you're creating a blog, an inventory management system, or a contact manager, the principles discussed in this chapter will help you approach the project methodically, ensuring it is both functional and maintainable.

12.1 Planning Your Own Mini-Project (e.g., Blog, Inventory, Contact Manager)

The first step in any software development project is planning. The most effective developers begin with a clear understanding of the project scope, its requirements, and the user experience they aim to create. When selecting your mini-project, consider its complexity and the skills you want to demonstrate. For example, building a blog system allows you to practice working with database models, user authentication, and CRUD (Create, Read, Update, Delete) functionality. An inventory system would require handling a more complex data model, with products, quantities, categories, and stock management. Similarly, a contact manager might involve managing user information, phone numbers, and email addresses, which can help you practice form handling and validation.

Once you have a project idea in mind, break it down into smaller, manageable tasks. For instance, if you're building a blog, your tasks might include setting up a database model for posts, creating user authentication, implementing CRUD operations, and designing a user-friendly interface. It's important to approach the project incrementally, starting with a basic prototype and gradually adding features. This ensures you maintain focus on the core functionality while leaving room for expansion.

To ensure your project is both feasible and well-scoped, consider the following questions during the planning phase:

- What is the core functionality of my project?
- What kind of data will my application handle?
- Who are the potential users, and how will they interact with the application?
- What technologies, tools, and libraries will I need to implement the features?

For example, if you're building a blog, your database schema might include tables for users and blog posts, with relationships like one-to-many (a user can write many posts). Understanding these relationships upfront will help you implement the backend with efficiency and clarity.

12.2 Implementing Your Chosen Idea

With the planning phase complete, the next step is to implement your mini-project. At this stage, you'll start writing code to bring your idea to life. It's important to follow the structure and guidelines established in the previous chapters while focusing on the specific features of your project. For instance, if you are building an inventory system, you'll need to focus on setting up models for inventory items, including attributes such as name, quantity, description, and price.

Let's consider an example where you're building a simple contact manager application. The core functionalities might include adding new contacts, displaying a list of contacts, editing existing contacts, and deleting contacts. Each of these features will require specific routes, templates, and form handling to ensure the data is properly managed.

Here is a simplified implementation outline for a contact manager:

Database Model (Using SQLAlchemy):

```
class Contact(db.Model):
    id = db.Column(db.Integer, primary_key=True)
    name = db.Column(db.String(100), nullable=False)
    phone = db.Column(db.String(20), nullable=False)
    email = db.Column(db.String(100), nullable=False)

    def __repr__(self):
        return f'<Contact {self.name}>'
```

Routes and Views:

```
@app.route('/contacts')
def contacts():
    all_contacts = Contact.query.all()
    return render_template('contacts.html',
contacts=all_contacts)

@app.route('/add_contact', methods=['GET', 'POST'])
def add_contact():
    if request.method == 'POST':
        name = request.form['name']
        phone = request.form['phone']
        email = request.form['email']
        new_contact = Contact(name=name, phone=phone,
email=email)
        db.session.add(new_contact)
        db.session.commit()
        return redirect(url_for('contacts'))
    return render_template('add_contact.html')
```

Templates (Using Jinja2):

The frontend templates will allow users to interact with the application, entering data and viewing existing entries. Here's an example of how you could display the list of contacts:

```
{% for contact in contacts %}
  <p>{{ contact.name }} - {{ contact.phone }} - {{
contact.email }}</p>
{% endfor %}
```

12.3 Code Cleanup and Refactoring

As your project progresses, it's important to periodically refactor your code to ensure it remains clean, efficient, and easy to maintain. Code refactoring involves restructuring the codebase without changing its functionality, making it easier to understand and improve performance.

Common techniques for refactoring in Flask projects include:

- **Modularization**: As your project grows, it can become increasingly difficult to manage everything within a single file. Flask's blueprint system, discussed in Chapter 8, allows you to break your application into smaller components. This is particularly helpful if your project involves multiple features or complex routes.
- **Separation of Concerns**: Ensure that your application's different layers (data models, routes, forms, templates) are separated into distinct files. This makes it easier to troubleshoot, extend, and scale your application.
- **Code Duplication**: Review your code for repeated logic and extract it into reusable functions. For example, if you find yourself repeating the same query to retrieve contacts or posts, consider placing that query logic into a separate function or service.

- **Error Handling**: Implement proper error handling to ensure that users are notified when something goes wrong, and ensure that your application can recover gracefully. Use Flask's error handling mechanisms, like `@app.errorhandler` to handle HTTP errors.

12.4 Documenting the Project (README)

A crucial part of software development is documenting your work. A well-written README provides clear instructions for anyone who wishes to run or contribute to your project. It helps other developers (and even your future self) understand the project's purpose, how to set it up, and how to use it.

A typical README for your Flask project might include the following sections:

1. **Project Title and Description**: A brief overview of the project's purpose.
2. **Installation Instructions**: Step-by-step instructions for setting up the project locally, including any dependencies (e.g., `Flask`, `SQLAlchemy`, etc.).
3. **Usage**: Instructions on how to run the application and interact with it (e.g., "Visit http://localhost:5000/contacts to view contacts").
4. **Contributing**: If your project is open for contributions, this section explains how others can help.
5. **License**: Information about the license under which the project is distributed (if applicable).

Example of a simple README:

Contact Manager

A Flask-based application for managing contacts.

Installation
1. Clone the repository:
```bash
git clone https://github.com/yourusername/contact-manager.git
```

2. Install the dependencies:
```bash
pip install -r requirements.txt
```

3. Set up the database:
```bash
flask db init
flask db migrate
flask db upgrade
```

Usage
4. Run the app:
```bash
flask run
```

Visit http://127.0.0.1:5000 to access the app.

12.5 Git and Version Control Basics

Version control is an essential practice in software development. It allows you to track changes, collaborate with other developers, and revert to previous versions if necessary. Git is the most widely used version control system, and it integrates seamlessly with platforms like GitHub and GitLab.

To get started with Git:

1. Initialize a Git repository:
```bash
git init
```

2. Add files to the staging area:
```bash
git add .
```

3. Commit changes with a meaningful message:
```bash
git commit -m "Initial commit"
```

4. Push your changes to a remote repository:
```bash
git push origin main
```

Using version control throughout the development process ensures that you have a clear history of changes, and it enables collaboration, making it an essential skill for any developer.

Conclusion

By the end of this chapter, you should have the skills to plan, implement, and refine a Flask mini-project that demonstrates both your understanding of Flask and your ability to build practical, real-world applications. From planning your project idea to documenting it and managing your code with Git, the steps covered in this chapter will equip you with the tools necessary to develop production-quality Flask applications. Through continuous learning and refining your approach, you will be able to enhance your problem-solving skills and create even more sophisticated applications in the future.

Bibliography

1. Flask Documentation. (n.d.). *Flask* (2.1.0). Retrieved April 10, 2025, from https://flask.palletsprojects.com/en/2.1.x/
2. Grinberg, M. (2018). *Flask web development: Developing web applications with Python* (2nd ed.). O'Reilly Media.
3. Python Software Foundation. (2023). *Flask tutorial: Introduction*. Retrieved April 10, 2025, from https://flask.palletsprojects.com/en/2.1.x/tutorial/
4. Bootstrap. (2023). *Bootstrap 5.3.5 documentation*. Retrieved April 10, 2025, from https://getbootstrap.com/docs/5.3/
5. Hunziker, R. (2017). *Flask by example: Unleashing the power of Flask*. Packt Publishing.
6. McKinney, W. (2018). *Python for data analysis: Data wrangling with pandas, numpy, and IPython* (2nd ed.). O'Reilly Media.
7. Cogan, D. (2021). *Modern Python development with Flask*. Apress.
8. Fitzgerald, M., & Sharda, R. (2022). *Web programming with Flask: An introduction to building full-stack web applications*. Springer.
9. Howell, J., & Sequeira, A. (2021). *Flask web development: Build scalable and maintainable web applications with Python*. Packt Publishing.
10. K, T., & MacDonald, A. (2020). *Web development with Flask and SQLAlchemy*. Apress.
11. Wilson, C. (2019). *Flask essentials: A practical guide to creating web applications using Flask and Python*. Packt Publishing.
12. Kumar, R. (2021). *Learn Flask and build web applications: Master Flask framework with hands-on examples*. Independently Published.
13. Lentin, M. (2019). *Flask web application development: Develop and deploy robust web applications using Flask*. Packt Publishing.
14. Bohn, A., & O'Hara, P. (2020). *Flask tutorial: Building simple web applications with Python*. Wiley.

15. Docker, Inc. (2021). *Deploying Flask applications with Docker*. Retrieved April 10, 2025, from https://www.docker.com/blog/deploying-flask-applications-with-docker/

About The Author

Early Life and Education

Mark John Lado was born on September 24, 1992, in Danao City,

Philippines. From an early age, he exhibited a keen interest in technology and education, which would later shape his career. He pursued his Bachelor of Science in Information Systems (BSIS) at Colegio de San Antonio de Padua, where he graduated with a strong foundation in technology and systems analysis. His academic journey continued as he earned a Master's degree in Information Technology (MIT) from the Northern Negros State College of Science and Technology in Sagay City, Philippines. Currently, he is pursuing his Doctorate in Information Technology at the State University of Northern Negros, reflecting his commitment to lifelong learning and professional growth.

Professional Career

Mark has built a diverse and impactful career in education and technology. He currently serves as an Instructor in the College of Technology and Engineering at Cebu Technological University, a role he has held since October 2022. Prior to this, he was a Faculty member in Business Education and Information Systems at Colegio de San Antonio de Padua from 2018 to 2022. His earlier roles include working as a Part-Time Information Technology Instructor at the University of the Visayas - Danao Branch and as an ICT Coordinator at Carmen Christian School Inc. in 2017.

Research and Innovation

Mark is an active researcher with a focus on applying technology to solve real-world problems. Some of his notable projects include:

1. "Development of a Microprocessor-Based Sensor Network for Monitoring Water Parameters in Tilapia Traponds"
2. "A Wireless Digital Public Address with Voice Alarm and Text-to-Speech Feature for Different Campuses", which was published in Globus: An International Journal of Management & IT

His research contributions highlight his dedication to innovation and his ability to bridge theoretical knowledge with practical applications.

Authorship and Publications

Mark is a prolific author, having written and published multiple books on technology topics. His works include:

1. Mastering CRUD with Flask in 5 Days; Build Python Web Applications - From Novice to...
2. Flask, PostgreSQL, and Bootstrap: Building Data-Driven Web Applications with CRUD...
3. From Model to Web App: A Comprehensive Guide to Building Data-Driven Web...
4. The Beginner's Guide Computer Systems; Principles, Practices, and Troubleshooting:...
5. Flask Web Framework Building Interactive Web Applications with SQLite Database: A...
6. Mastering PC Troubleshooting & Operating Systems: The Modern Landscape of PC...
7. Mastering Flask in 5 Days; From Zero to Deployment: Building Your First Web App:...
8. Data Modeling and Process Analysis; Essential for Technology Analysts and AI...
9. The Echo of the Past; Information Networks from Stone to Silicon and Beyond AI: How...

10. Cybersecurity Essentials Protecting Your Digital Life, Data, and Privacy in a...
11. Mastering PC Troubleshooting and Operating Systems: The Future-Ready...
12. From Idea to Manuscript: A Step-by-Step Guide to Writing Your Nonfiction Book
13. Microprocessor Magic: Unlocking the Potential of Building Projects from Scratch
14. Data Modeling and Process Analysis: A Comprehensive Guide – Volume I
15. Python Data Science Essentials: A Comprehensive Guide to Mastering...
16. Mastering PC Troubleshooting and Operating Systems: A Comprehensive Guide
17. Cybersecurity Confidence: 8 Steps to Master Digital Security and Boost Productivity
18. Embedded Systems: From Historical Development to Modern-Day Applications

These books are widely recognized and serve as valuable resources for students, hobbyists, and professionals in the IT field. His publications are available on platforms like Amazon and ThriftBooks, further extending his reach and impact

Certifications and Professional Development

Mark has pursued several certifications to enhance his expertise, including:

- Computer Hardware Servicing from Cebu Technological University
- Consumer Electronics Servicing from TESDA

These certifications underscore his commitment to continuous professional development and staying updated with emerging technological trends.

Contributions to IT Education

As an active member of the Philippine Society of Information Technology Educators (PSITE), Mark contributes to advancing IT education standards in the Philippines. His teaching, research, and authorship have made him a respected figure in the academic and IT communities. He is known for his adaptability to emerging technologies, such as AI-driven systems and cybersecurity, ensuring that his work remains relevant and impactful.

Personal Interests

Outside of his professional life, Mark enjoys reading books, spending time at the beach, and engaging in physical activities like inline skating and biking. These hobbies not only help him unwind but also contribute to his overall well-being and creativity.

Legacy and Impact

Mark John Lado's dedication to education, research, and professional excellence has made him a valuable asset to the IT community. His contributions have empowered countless students and professionals, preparing them for the challenges of a rapidly evolving technological landscape. His unwavering passion for technology and continuous pursuit of learning ensure that his legacy will endure for years to come.

For more details about his work, you can visit his official website https://markjohnlado.com/

or explore his publications on Amazon Author Page https://www.amazon.com/stores/author/B0BZM8PM6R

I highly recommend reading this book to further enhance your skills and deepen your understanding of the subject.

https://a.co/d/ahv6VWa

https://a.co/d/b1W3F8n

https://a.co/d/izTWNbO

https://a.co/d/6HHyUFk